Natural Disaster

TORNADO

Edited by: Pallabi B. Tomar, Hitesh Iplani

Managing editor: Tapasi De

Designed by: Vijesh Chahal, Anil Kumar, Rohit Kumar

Illustrated by: Suman S. Roy, Tanoy Choudhury

Colouring done by: Vinay Kumar, Kiran Kumari & Pradeep Kumar

CONTENTS

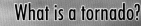

What is a tornado?

A tornado is a violent, column-like system of rapidly-rotating air that is in contact with both the surface of the earth and a cumulonimbus cloud. Most tornadoes are funnel-shaped. Although tornadoes are short-lived (they usually last for a few minutes), they can be very destructive and even deadly.

Tornadoes form in thunderstorms when unstable hot air near the ground rises and meets cooler air above in thunder clouds. The winds inside a tornado spirals upwards with a lot of speed and power. It creates an internal vacuum that sucks up anything it passes over. When the funnel touches a structure, the fierce winds have the ability to tear it apart.

The word 'tornado' comes from the Spanish or Portuguese verb tornar, meaning 'to turn.' A tornado is also commonly referred to as a 'twister'. Some tornadoes are clearly visible, while rain or nearby low-hanging clouds obscure others. Occasionally, tornadoes develop so rapidly that little, if any, advance warning is possible.

Astonishing fact

The tornado is the most violent of all Earth's storms.

Causes of tornadoes

Tornadoes are produced when two differing air masses meet. When cooler polar air masses meet warm and moist tropical air masses, the potential for severe weather is created. The warm southern winds try to rise, but the cold northern air blocks them. This clash causes the warm, trapped air to rotate horizontally between the two air masses. At the same time, the sun heats the earth below, warming more air that continues to try and rise. Finally, the rising warm wind becomes strong enough to force itself up through the colder air layer.

Astonishing fact

In Oklahoma, a small herd of cattle were sucked up by a tornado and carried across the countryside, before being set down safe and sound.

When this occurs, the cold air on top begins to sink, sending the rising warm wind spinning upward. The warm winds rotate faster and faster in a high column forming an updraft. When the updraft is strong, the column can rise to heights of 16 km or more, twisting at speeds of up to 160 km an hour. The rotating winds produce strong storm clouds about 21,336 m high, sometimes spreading 16 km wide.

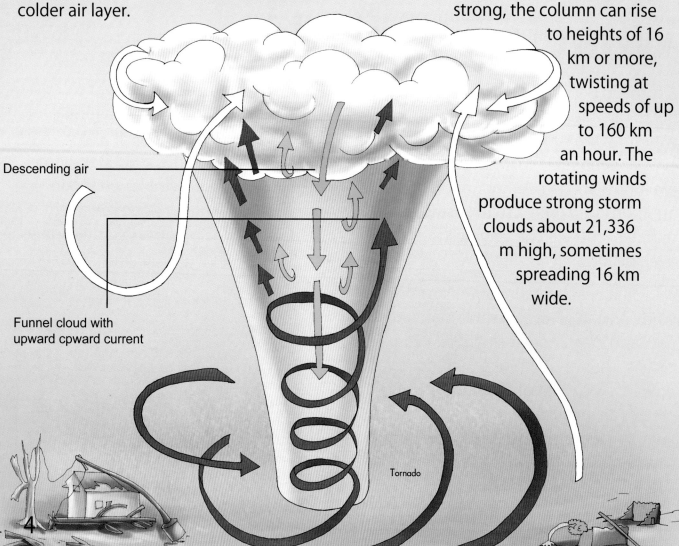

Descending air

Funnel cloud with upward cpward current

Tornado

Most tornadoes come from severe thunderstorms that have air in rotation within them. These are called supercells. It is seen that about one amongst a thousand storms becomes a supercell and one among five or six supercells becomes a tornado.

The rotating updraft of air is known as a mesocyclone. The mesocyclone is the part of the supercell that draws large amounts of air into the storm system. Within the mesocyclone, vertical wind shear can cause a mass of air to start spinning. When air spins, it creates a low pressure area. The low pressure area draws in even more air into the growing twister.

Supercells are very large, rotating thunderstorms. They can live a very long time and generate several tornadoes. Tornadoes formed from supercell thunderstorms are more damaging partly because of their duration. One kind of supercell creates huge amounts of precipitation and large, damaging hail. The other kind produces less precipitation and large hail but makes tornadoes. Squall lines form from the border between warm and cold fronts or from a storm that has split.

Astonishing fact

Most of the world's destructive tornadoes occur during the summer in the mid-western states of the US.

Features of a tornado

All tornadoes have a funnel-shape cloud that is their distinctive characteristic. They maybe horn shape, a perfectly straight funnel, a helix screw shape, thin and ropey in appearance, a vertical cylinder or so wide that they appear to be a large black cloud, touching the ground. Pairs of tornadoes that rotate around each other are common. Large tornadoes may also produce several smaller tornadoes that travel along with them. Two tornadoes may even travel from different origin points, meet, merge and become one massive tornado.

Tornadoes vary considerably in colour. When they are first forming or initially reaching the ground, they may almost be invisible. Once in contact with the ground, the vortex maybe white, bluish gray, brown, dark gray, or almost black. At night, a tornado in the air passing over community may glow red with electrical sparks shooting out from it.

Astonishing fact

Rescue workers have compared the devastation left behind by a tornado to a bomb blast.

Tornadoes vary in size as well. They are on average between 130-170 m wide and can travel between 35-90 km per hour along the ground. These tornadoes usually last for several minutes and can cut a path of destruction a couple of kilometres long. The largest tornadoes that are nearly 2 km across are the most destructive but they are very rare. Their winds can exceed 400 km per hour and can travel at 110 km per hour.

A tornado can form very quickly, sometimes in a minute or less. It can travel across the ground at high speeds and then just as suddenly vanish. They can kill in a matter of seconds. Most tornadoes last less than twenty minutes and travel less than 24 km. However, superstorms sometimes occur, travelling over 160 km before they are exhausted. Although they don't occur very often, they are responsible for 20% of all tornado casualties.

Small tornadoes sometimes form on the edge of bigger tornadoes.

Observers near the vicinity of a tornado have reported several different sounds emanating from the funnel cloud. The most common sound reported was a constant, dull rumbling like that made by train. Some have reported a high pitched sound like a jet engine, while others have reported a sound like one makes when blowing a bottle.

Tornado life cycle

A tornado has five stages that it undergoes during its life cycle.

1. A rotating column of air forms within a cumulonimbus cloud and extends towards the ground. This can be seen as a rotating funnel dropping out from the bottom of the cloud towards the ground. Until the rotating funnel reaches the ground, it is called a 'funnel cloud.'

2. When the rotating column of air reaches the ground, it is then called a 'tornado.' The funnel can be seen touching the ground and sometimes dust and debris can be seen swirling about on the ground before the tornado actually touches down.

3. Once the tornado reaches 'maturity,' it is almost always vertical and touching the ground. At this point, anything the tornado encounters is severely damaged or destroyed.

4. During the 'shrinking stage,' the funnel becomes narrow and less vertical. In this stage, the damage path becomes smaller.

5. When a tornado reaches the 'decaying stage,' the funnel is stretched into a rope shape. The visible portion becomes twisted and finally dissipates.

Tornadoes have hit places even in big cities like Brooklyn.

Types of tornadoes

There are many different types of tornadoes. They can range in shape from narrow and rope-like, narrow or fat cylinders or cone or wedge-shaped. They also form in different situations.

Supercell tornadoes

This type of tornado originates from supercell thunderstorms. The main characteristic of these storms is the presence of a thick upwardly drawn air current in a constant rotational motion, which is called mesocyclone. The tornadoes that are evolved out of these storms are big in size and are in the shape of a wedge. Supercell tornadoes tend to keep contact with the ground for a very long time and are extremely fierce in nature, with winds blowing at a speed above 321 km/hr!

Waterspout

Waterspouts are simply tornadoes that exist over a body of water. They are often much weaker than land-based twisters due to atmospheric differences.

Waterspouts are able to pick up the water and swirl it in its funnel. In some occasions, waterspouts have picked up tadpoles, lizards and fish which eventually rained down from the sky once the waterspout diminished.

These often occur in tropical regions where there are oceans and lakes. Ships out on the open seas have reported seeing up to as many as 30 waterspouts in one day!

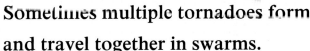

Astonishing fact

Sometimes multiple tornadoes form and travel together in swarms.

Waterspout

Landspout

The other name of landspout tornado is **dust-tube tornado**. This type of tornado is of much lesser intensity as compared to a supercell tornado and they are of shorter duration. It does not have any kind of association with mesocyclone. Even though it is a weaker form of tornado, it yields quite strong winds that are capable of inflicting massive damage. Usually, the smooth condensation funnel of landspout is not in touch with the ground. However, when it makes contact, a thin layer cloud of dust is formed.

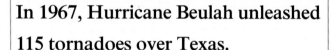

Astonishing fact

In 1967, Hurricane Beulah unleashed 115 tornadoes over Texas.

Dust devil

Dry, hot, clear days on the desert or over dry land can bring about dust devils. Generally forming in the hot sun during the late morning or early afternoon hours, these mostly harmless whirlwinds are triggered by light desert breezes that create a swirling plume of dust with speeds rarely over 112 km/hr. They are not associated with a thunderstorm (or any cloud), and are usually weaker than the weakest tornado. In most cases, dust devils are no more than 3 m wide and less 100 m high.

Typically, the life cycle of a dust devil is a few minutes or less, although they can last much longer. Although usually harmless, they have been known to cause minor damage. They can blow vehicles off the road and could damage your eyes by blowing dust into them.

Dust Devil

Astonishing fact

In 1981, a tornado that swept through the Italian City of Ancona lifted a sleeping baby from its baby carriage and set it down unharmed on the ground.

Firewhirls

Gustnado

A gustnado can be defined as a gust front tornado. It is a weak tornado that does not last for a long period of time. Technically, there is no link between the cloud base and the circulation of the wind. Hence, it is not considered as a tornado. It is a temporary whirl of dust and debris, confined to a small area with a heavy rotational wind. They look similar to dust devils.

Firewhirls

Firewhirls are often referred to as fire tornadoes, firenadoes or firedevils. The heat formed by a wildfire or volcanic eruption causes firewhirls. It consists of a column of rotational smoke or fire which looks like a tornado. The wind speed of firewhirls is usually above 160 km/hr.

Gustnado

Sizes of tornadoes

Tornadoes come in three different sizes, each with different characteristics. The three sizes are— weak, strong, and violent. Their size is based on how large the tornado is as well as the time that the tornado lasts.

A **weak tornado** is the most common type of tornado and makes up 69% of all tornadoes. The least number of deaths happen from this type of tornado, and the longest they can last is a little more than 10 minutes. Winds within this category of tornado are less than 161 km/hr. Weak tornadoes are part of the first two categories of the Fujita Scale (F0 & F1).

Damage from a weak tornado can include broken tree branches and peeling off the roofs from houses and buildings.

Astonishing fact

A heavy chicken house was picked up by a tornado and stuck between two trees. The hens were found the next day sitting on their eggs in the chicken house, with no windows broken, as though nothing had happened!

Strong tornadoes include 29% of all tornadoes. This type of tornado causes 30% of all deaths from tornadoes. Wind speeds for strong tornadoes are between 177-330 km/hr. These tornadoes can last 20 minutes or even longer. Demolished homes and overturned trains are parts of the damage that could happen from a strong tornado.

While a **violent tornado** is the least common, it is very deadly. Violent tornadoes make up 70% of all tornado deaths. This type of tornado can last over an hour. Wind speeds for violent tornadoes are typically greater than 330 km/hr. A violent tornado is part of the last two categories on the Fujita Scale (F4 & F5). These tornadoes can do a lot of damage, including throwing cars and picking up well built houses and carrying them for miles.

Some people in ancient times thought that dust devils were ghosts.

When and where do they occur?

United States has by far the most tornadoes in the world. It averages 1,000 tornadoes a year. Tornadoes have been observed on all continents except Antarctica. Outside United States, Argentina and Bangladesh have the next most occurrences.

The geography of the central U.S. is uniquely suited to bring together all the ingredients for tornado formation. With the Rocky Mountains to the west, the Gulf of Mexico in the south, and a ground that slopes downward from west to east, this area has become know as 'Tornado Alley,' averaging more than 500 tornadoes occurring annually.

Tornadoes can form at any time of a day, although the most common time is between 3pm and 9 pm. Spring and summer are the most common times of a year for tornado formation.

> Tornadoes occur mostly in May. They occur the least in the months of January and February.

Tornado Alley

Tornadoes form all over the world, but some areas are more prone to tornadoes than others. USA gets a lot of tornadoes, about 1,000 each year on an average. In USA, tornadoes have formed in every state, but **Tornado Alley** has a very high number of very destructive tornadoes.

The geography of the central part of United States, known as the Great Plains, is suited to bring all of the ingredients together to form tornadoes. More than 500 tornadoes typically occur in this area every year and that is why it is commonly known as 'Tornado Alley'.

Tornado Alley extends from central Texas northward to Illinois and Indiana. The heart of Tornado Alley includes parts of Texas, Oklahoma, Kansas, Nebraska, eastern Colorado, and South Dakota. Less intense areas of Tornado Alley include parts of Arkansas, Louisiana, Mississippi, Iowa, Tennessee, Kentucky, Wisconsin, and Minnesota.

People who live in Tornado Alley are aware that tornadoes pose a potential danger for them. Building codes in these areas require that new buildings have strong roofs and a foundation that is tethered to the structure. Many people have storm cellars, underground shelters that protect people from a tornado. Many areas have neighbourhood tornado sirens that warn people of imminent tornadoes.

Astonishing fact

Many houses in tornado alley have strong basement shelters.

On average, 100 people are killed by tornadoes each year.

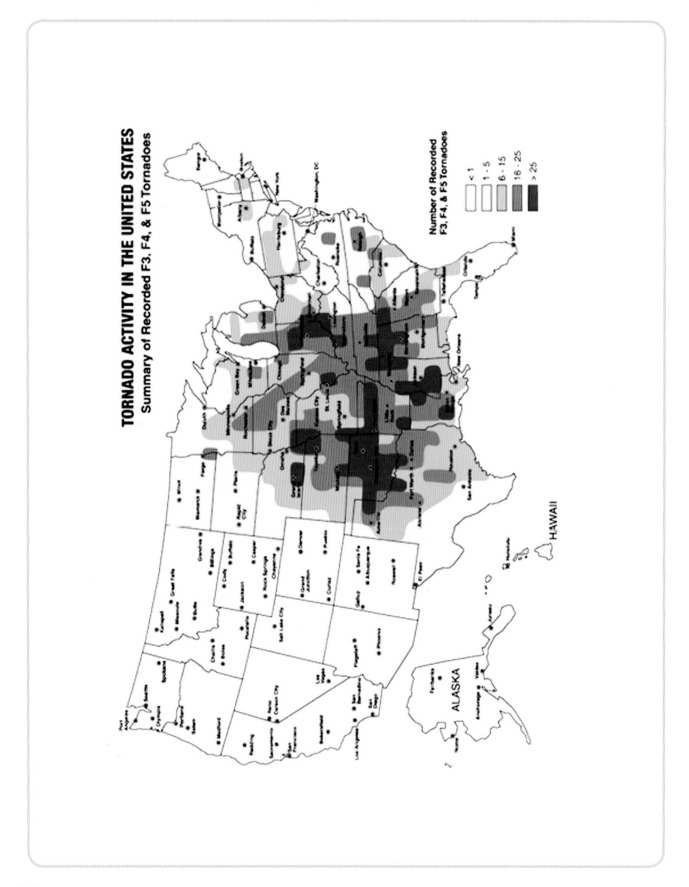

TORNADO ACTIVITY IN THE UNITED STATES
Summary of Recorded F3, F4, & F5 Tornadoes

Number of Recorded
F3, F4, & F5 Tornadoes

< 1
1 - 5
6 - 15
16 - 25
> 25

ALASKA

HAWAII

How are tornadoes measured?

Before 1971, there was no way for scientists to rank tornadoes by their strength. How big the tornado looked had no bearing on how strong it actually was. In 1971, Professor Tetsuya Theodore Fujita came up with a system to rank tornadoes according to how much damage they cause. This was called the **Fujita Scale**. As of February 1, 2007, a new scale for rating the strength of tornadoes is being used. It is called the **Enhanced Fujita Scale**. The Enhanced Fujita Scale or EF Scale has six categories from zero to five, with EF5 being the highest degree of damage. The

Tetsuya Theodore Fujita

Scale was used for the first time as three separate tornadoes took place in central Florida early on February 2, 2007.

ORIGINAL FUJITA SCALE		ENHANCED FUJITA SCALE	
F5	261-318 mph	EF5	+200 mph
F4	207-260 mph	EF4	166-200 mph
F3	158-206 mph	EF3	136-165 mph
F2	113-157 mph	EF2	111-135 mph
F1	73-112 mph	EF1	86-110 mph
F0	<73 mph	EF0	65-85 mph

Tracking of tornadoes

Tornadoes are extremely difficult if not impossible to forecast. Meteorologists can forecast conditions most likely to induce tornado formation but cannot predict when and where a tornado will happen. Forecasters can predict severe thunderstorms and the possibility for tornadoes but it's not a certain fact that a tornado will hit. Based on previous information, tornado statistics and climatology data, meteorologists can issue watches and warnings for tornadoes. With increasingly advanced technology, storm chases are improving storm and tornado tracking. An increase in the number of reported tornadoes recently has been due to better technology in detection and tracking, such as **Doppler Radar**.

A National Oceanic and Atmospheric Administration (NOAA) weather alert radio receiver, equipped with a warning siren, can warn of an impending tornado when people are sleeping.

Doppler Radar

Tornadoes are very dangerous so it's important to know when they may form so people can take shelter. Trained weather spotters are often on alert to look for tornadoes and notify local weather agencies when severe weather is occurring or predicted to be imminent. In the United States, Skywarn spotters fulfil this role. In addition, some individuals known as storm chasers, enjoy pursuing thunderstorms and tornadoes to explore their many visual and scientific aspects.

A tornado always rotates either clockwise or counter clockwise. A large amount of dust is thus raised due to these cyclonic winds.

Storm chasers

Storm chasers are different than storm spotters. Chasers travel around Tornado Alley looking for severe storms and tornadoes. This area in the 'Great Plains' is the best for chasing because of the frequency of storms and also because of the relatively flat ground. There aren't as many hills and trees to block a chaser's view of a storm. All kinds of people are chasers. Most people chase storms because they are interested in meteorology and because they want to see severe weather up close. Others are interested in taking pictures or videos of the storms.

Storm chasers

Damages

Tornadoes can cause a damage of millions and even billions of dollars. They are large columns of rotating wind that can carry debris for miles. Tornadoes can only lift heavy objects like houses, trains and cars over short distances, but paper items have been found even 160 km away from where they were originally lifted by a tornado. Furthermore, aircraft pilots have reported seeing debris fluttering through the air at high altitudes near the thunderstorm where a tornado was occurring.

Tornadoes typically produce winds up to and over 400 km/hr. About 1,000 tornadoes are reported across the United States in an average year, causing about 80 deaths and over 1,500 injuries. Approximately, 45 percent of these deaths are of people living in mobile homes. A lot of injuries result from objects being tossed around by a tornado.

Astonishing fact

A strong tornado can pick up a house and move it down the block.

Better safe than sorry

Tornado safety tips

Tornadoes are one of nature's most powerful and destructive forces. Here's some advice on how to prepare for a tornado and what to do if you're caught in a twister's path.

1. Determine the best locations for shelter at home and work. The safest location is always a basement. If you can't go underground, find a small interior room or hallway on the lowest level of the building.

2. Prepare an emergency supply kit. Experts recommend that each person has supplies for at least three days, including bottled water, food and a first-aid kit. Make sure you have tools such as a can opener, utility knife, wrench, whistle, battery-powered radio, flashlights and batteries. Each person will need blankets, clothing, rain gear and heavy-soled shoes. Lastly, put away some cash for emergency.

3. Know how your community sends its warnings. If it's a siren, stay inside and take cover. Know where the designated shelters are in the buildings where you and your family spend time.

Astonishing fact

Knives and forks have been found embedded in tree trunks flung from a tornado!

Tornado safety kit

4. Know the difference between a 'watch' and a 'warning.' There's a big difference in the danger level between the two terms used during stormy weather. A 'watch' simply means that conditions are favorable for a tornado to develop. Be alert, but you don't need to take shelter. If there's a warning, a tornado has been spotted. When a warning is posted for your area, take shelter immediately.

5. Get in position. Once you're in your shelter, find a strong piece of furniture, such as a table and stay under it. Curl into a ball on the floor, and lock your hands behind your head to protect it from flying debris. If you can't find a table to get under, crouch under a door frame because the beams will offer some protection.

6. Stay away from windows; pieces of glass can be deadly. You can eliminate this risk if you make sure your shelter area is free of windows. If this isn't possible, protect yourself with a heavy blanket.

Astonishing fact

In 1983, lightning struck right next to five tornado chasers. Luckily they all lived.

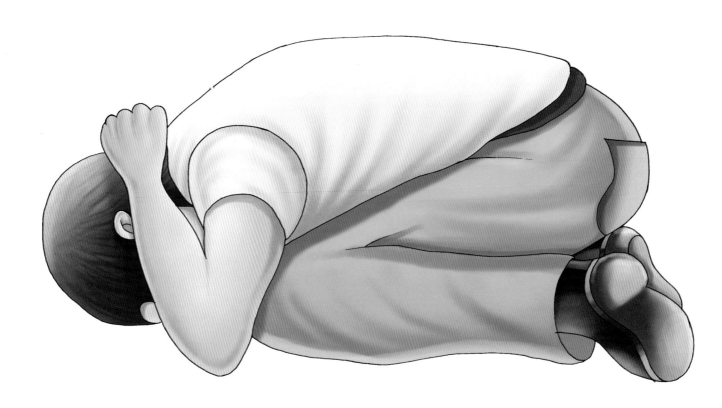

7. If you are in a vehicle, never try to outrun a tornado. Get out of your vehicle and try to get inside a building. If there isn't time, lie down flat in a ditch or any low-lying area away from the vehicle. Use your hands and arms to protect your head.

8. After the storm has passed, treat injuries with your first-aid kit, but don't attempt to move anyone who is severely injured. Use the phone only for emergencies, such as calling for an ambulance. Then, listen to the radio for emergency information. If the building you are in is damaged, beware of broken glass and downed power lines as you evacuate. Check on neighbours who might need assistance, but otherwise stay out of the way so that emergency crews can do their work.

9. Beware of fire hazards. Never strike a match until you're sure you haven't had a gas leak. Anything that holds gas can burst and be vulnerable to explosions if you see or smell leakage after a storm. If you think there might be a gas leak, open all doors and get out of the house. Also watch out for severed electrical wires which can spark debris piles. Check appliances to see if they are emitting smoke or sparks.

Astonishing fact

A Tornado can sometimes hop along its path. It can destroy one house and leave the house next door untouched!

Deadliest tornadoes in history

Saturia–Manikganj Sadar tornado

The Saturia–Manikganj Sadar tornado was a catastrophic tornado that struck the Manikganj district of Bangladesh on April 26, 1989. Causing approximately 1,300 fatalities, it was the deadliest tornado in recorded history.

The tornado struck at around 6:30 pm local time and moved east from the Daulatpur area into the areas of Saturia and Manikganj Sadar—a region that had been suffering from a severe drought. The storm spanned a path that was about 16 km long and about 1.6 km wide. Though confined to a relatively small geographic region and brief in duration, it completely destroyed all buildings within an area of roughly 6 square km. Towns lay in ruins, and thousands of residents were left homeless. In addition, thousands of trees were uprooted and blown away. The Saturia–Manikganj Sadar tornado was only one of the numerous devastating storms to hit Bangladesh in recent history.

The Tri-State tornado

The 1925 Tri-State Tornado was the single most deadly tornado in United State's history. It was a massive tornado that ripped through parts of south-eastern Missouri, southern Illinois and south-western Indiana. At 1:01pm on March 18th 1925, the Great Tri-State tornado started out from the Ozarks in south-eastern Missouri, headed eastward through southern Illinois and lifted in southwestern Indiana after a duration of three and a half hours. The tornado travelled at an average speed of 99 km/hr which is approximately double the speed of an average tornado. The tornado was rated as a F5 on the Fujita Scale.

In total, there were 695 deaths and over 2000 people were injured. The distance of 352 km is the longest recorded in history. It destroyed 15,000 homes, and damaged more than 424 square km (almost 50 times more than the average tornado). Property damage was worth $16.5 million and would be almost $2 billion at today's prices!

A tornado makes a deafening roar as it passes by.

The Great Natchez tornado

The second worst tornado in U.S. history hit Natchez in 1840. It killed 317 people and injured 109. This is the only recorded tornado in the U.S. that killed more people than were injured.

Shortly after noon on May 7, 1840, a mile-wide tornado slammed into Natchez, Mississippi, a city on the Mississippi River, about 241 km north of New Orleans. The storm was loaded with all kinds of debris it had picked up along its path. No one expected it and no one was warned of its approach even though the sounds of its destruction farther down the river could be heard in Natchez. Unlike the present time, there was no national weather service to alert people to an approaching storm and there were none of the things that individuals could have used to warn others, two-way radios, telephones, or cell phones. As the tornado struck Natchez, banks, homes, stores, steamboats, and other vessels were completely destroyed. Houses burst open. Three hundred and seventeen people lost their lives. It was the second most deadly tornado in U.S. history.

North American Tornado Swarm (1974)

Known as the **Super Outbreak**, 148 tornadoes touched down in an area stretching from Ontario Canada in the north to Alabama in the south over a period of two days.

It was the worst tornado outbreak in U.S. history with 148 twisters touching down in 11 states. And before it was over 16 hours later, 330 people were dead and 5,484 were injured in a damage path covering more than 2,500 miles.

In Illinois and Indiana, several groups of thunderstorms and supercells (which cause tornadoes) began to form. These intense storms moved towards the Ohio Valley and in the late afternoon, it spawned four F5 tornadoes between 4:30pm to 6:30pm on April 4, 1974. This was due to three supercells which hit central and southern Ohio, southern Indiana and northern Kentucky. Some of these areas had already experienced tornadoes on 1 and 2, April.

At the same time, thunderstorms developed in an area which spread from the Appalachians to Georgia. On the evening of April 3, storm activity in the south began to escalate. Several tornadoes hit central Tennessee, eastern Kentucky and northern Alabama.

Meanwhile in the north, more supercells developed over southern Michigan and northern Indiana. Additional tornadoes touched down, including Windsor Ontario, between 6:00pm and 10:00pm.

On the morning of April 4, the southern storm moved up towards the Appalachians and generated several tornadoes in the southeastern states.

By the end of April 4 1974, the Super Outbreak produced 148 twisters.

St. Louis Tornado

One of the deadliest tornadoes ever to strike in the United States happened in St. Louis on May 27, 1896. Two of the tornadoes, both F4 in strength, impacted St. Louis and East St. Louis.

At 6:30 pm, May 27, 1896, two F4 tornadoes touched down near and on St. Louis, Missouri, almost simultaneously. One passed over the city and moved in a southeasterly direction, leveling entire farms in such communities as Richview and Irvington sixty miles east of St. Louis. The other, a much more powerful tornado, was the **third deadliest tornado** in U.S. history, responsible for the deaths of 255 people on both sides of the river before it

finally petered out in East St. Louis, Illinois. In East St. Louis, the swath of the tornado narrowed and, as so often happens in such circumstances, the funnel's speed and power increased. Devastation was complete and 118 people died. Two million dollars worth of damage had been done in east St. Louis.

Tupelo-Gainesville Outbreak

A vast storm system raced across the south-eastern states on April 5-6, 1936, spawning at least seventeen destructive tornadoes, with much loss of life as well as property damage. The storms also produced widespread destructive flooding across the region.

The greatest tornado damage and loss of life occurred in Tupelo, Mississippi, and Gainesville, Georgia. Total deaths for this outbreak reached at least 450. The Tupelo tornado was the fourth deadliest (with an estimated 216 dead) and the Gainesville tornado the fifth deadliest (with an estimated 203 dead) – in U.S. history.

The Waco Tornado

The Waco Tornado on May 11, 1953 tops the list as the deadliest tornado in Texas since 1900. The violent and deadly twister ripped through the downtown area, killing and injuring hundreds.

The tornado touched down around 4:10 pm south-west of Waco, near the town of Lorena in McLennan County. After destroying a home north of Lorena, the tornado moved north-northeast toward Waco.

The tornado wreaked havoc through the downtown area. Eyewitness reports indicated very heavy rain falling at the time of the tornado, making it difficult for people in downtown Waco to see the twister coming and taking action.

The twister continued plowing north-east of Waco, finally dissipating near the community of Axtell after a 37 km long path of destruction.

Tornadoes are most frequently reported east of the Rocky Mountains during spring and summer months.

Killing 114 and injuring 597, the Waco tornado holds the title of the deadliest tornado in Texas history since 1900. Striking the heart of the downtown area at the end of the work day, many people were caught unaware of the impending severe weather. 30 people were killed when a 6-storey furniture store collapsed, while 5 others were killed in their cars. The destruction was so massive, survivors waited up to 14 hours to be rescued and some bodies could not be recovered for several days following the disaster.

Tornadoes can accompany tropical storms and hurricanes as they move onto land.

Test Your MEMORY

1. What is a tornado?

2. Write the causes of tornadoes.

3. Write two characteristics of tornadoes.

4. Describe the lifecycle of a tornado.

5. Describe two types of tornadoes.

6. Write about the sizes of tornadoes.

7. Where do tornadoes occur?

8. What is Tornado Alley?

9. How are tornadoes measured?

10. Write two tornado safety tips.

11. Name the deadliest tornado in history.

12. Name the most deadly tornado in United States history.

Index